how to draw
manga

how to draw
manga

Katy Coope

SCHOLASTIC INC.

New York   Toronto   London   Auckland   Sydney

Mexico City   New Delhi   Hong Kong   Buenos Aires

Published by Scholastic Inc. 557 Broadway,
New York, NY 10012.

Scholastic and associated logos are
trademarks of Scholastic Inc.

ISBN 0-439-31745-2

This book was designed and produced by
D&S Books Limited
Kerswell, Parkham Ash
Bideford, Devon, EX39 5PR. UK

Creative director: Sarah King
Editor: Anna Southgate
Project editor: Clare Haworth-Maden
Designer: Axis Design

Printed in China

Contents

Getting Started

Getting Started

To draw Manga, you'll need some basic equipment, like pencils and pens. There is quite a choice of materials you can buy, so it's a good idea to experiment a bit to see what works best for you. A guide to the different materials is included in the last chapter.

The most basic thing you should know when drawing is that almost everything can be broken down into a group of spheres, tubes, and boxes. A head can be made from a sphere or an egg shape, and more complicated things like a hand, or even a whole character, are simply a big collection of shapes. For instance, this hand and cute critter...

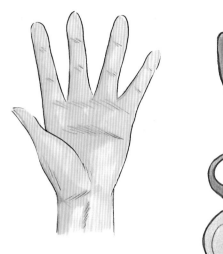

...are made from these simple shapes:

Getting Started

Artists use these shapes to help them draw. What they end up with may look very neat and finished, but before they get to that point, there's usually a lot of planning in pencil with shapes and guidelines. All you get to see are the lines the artist chooses to keep. Much of the original working - the parts the artist doesn't want - will have been erased along the way. For instance, this picture...

...looked like this before it was inked and the pencil lines were erased.

Drawing a Basic Face

We have to start somewhere, and this seems as good a place as any. We're going to draw an easy face, from the front, looking straight at you. Try and copy these steps as closely as you can, and work lightly up to step 7. This picture might not be in the style of your favorite Anime or Manga, but we're just getting the basics here.

In this case, the head is based on a circle instead of the usual egg shape. We'll move on to the other kind in the next chapter. Remember, you have to walk before you can run, so copy what I do here as best as you can.

2 Now start the eyes as they are in the picture. They should begin on the lower eye line and have their highest point on the top one. In most pictures, the slight point on the outside of each eye should be on the center line.

1 First, start with a circle. Draw a cross cutting it into quarters and add the other two horizontal lines as shown. We'll call these the eye lines.

3 See the kind of backward "J" shape in the eyes? That's the iris. Imagine it as an oval, with the top part hidden under the top of the eye and a gap in the side in the direction the light is coming from. (Here, the light is in the top right-hand corner. It's a common place to put the highlight.) Also, put in that little line on the center line. That's going to be the nose.

Drawing a Basic Face

4 Finish the shine in the eye with another curve, as if there was a white oval in the upper corner of the eye. Now it's time to make this circle look more like a head. Draw a slightly curved line from where the top eye line meets the circle, down to a little way in from where the lower eye line meets the circle. Draw lines from there to about the point the vertical center line meets the circle for the chin, as shown. Also, add a little ''c'' shape next to the nose line. This is for a shadow. After that, draw the eyebrows. They're hardly ever in a straight line, and here they curve down a bit toward the middle.

5 Now finish the eyes. Add another little oval in the opposite corner to the big one and draw in the pupils. In most cases, part of the pupil will be covered by the shine ovals. You'll also want to add that little curve for the darker part of the eye. Next, add the mouth, about halfway between the nose and chin. It might look like a straight line, but don't be tempted to use a ruler.

Now that you have the main features, add the ears and neck. I decided to give this guy a bandana, so draw that in, too. There's no right or wrong place to put the headgear and hair, so try to imagine where they would look best. Remember that hair never lies flat on the head.

Now determine which lines are going to be inked. I decided I wanted the guy to have little locks of hair in front of his ears, so I drew them in as well. Put a few lines on the bandana near the knot, and maybe shade in the pupil and shade in the eye. Make sure the lines you want are easy to see. If not, go over them a little darker, but not too hard, otherwise you won't be able to erase them.

Draw in the curl of hair wherever you feel it should go. If it's not how you want it, erase it, and try again. Add the rest of his hair and the ends of his bandana as well.

With all that done, it's time to break out the pen. I used a medium one (0.3 or 0.5) for most of it and an extra-fine one (0.1) for the finer detail on the eye, mouth, and nose.

You might want to experiment on a scrap piece of paper before you use it on your pencil work. I added some diagonal "blush lines" around the nose. Do these lightly and quickly. Once you have all the lines you want to keep inked, it's time to erase the pencil lines. And hey! You've got your first face. Of course, there's one more thing you can do...

Drawing a Basic Face

9 ...and that's color it in! I used colored pencils for this. If you want to try shading, remember that things cast shadows (so it'll be darker in those places). You'll learn more about that later. You can use whatever colors you want for the hair, bandana, and eyes, though, with the black eyebrows, I find that dark roots make the hair look more natural. I used red for the bandana because it's a nice, bold color, but any color will look just fine. When you've finished, don't forget to sign your name to show who drew it. It's your picture, after all!

So there you have it,

your first face.

Great job!

Drawing Chibi Characters

Now that you've drawn your first face, try drawing a few more till you get the hang of it. Once you feel you've got it, it'll be time to move on to drawing your first full figure.

One of the basic figures to start with is what's known as a Chibi figure. (It's also sometimes called Plushie-styled.) There are many different ways of drawing Chibi characters, but one of the most common is the "three-heads-high" method, which is what we're going to be using. For this project, I've drawn the new lines in blue to make them easier to see.

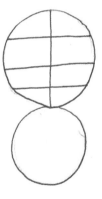

1. Start off with one circle for the head and another one about the same size underneath that. About one circle-height under that, draw a line. This is where the feet will go. On the head, draw the same guidelines that you drew when you were drawing the face. Because a Chibi figure has big eyes, the eye lines should cut the circle into quarters (or eighths, if you count the vertical line). On the bottom line, draw two half-circles for the feet.

2. Draw the first part of the eyes, and the bangs. Start to make the circle more face-shaped by putting in the curve between the eye lines. Do roughly the same thing to the body circle, but taller and thinner, as you can see in the picture. Draw in his legs and a couple of little half-circles for his hands.

3. Add some more detail to the eyes, and draw in the eyebrows and mouth. Give him a chin, and some spiked hair. Add his neck, and draw his clothes. Use the lines you already have to guide you. I gave him a T-shirt over a pullover, and some baggy jeans. I also gave him a longer piece of hair in front of his ears. Oh, and I drew in what you'd be able to see of his ears as well.

Drawing Chibi Characters

4 Finish off the hair and eyes, and add some little diagonal blush lines. Chibi pictures often don't have a nose when drawn from the front, and only have a very small one from other angles. Finish off his feet and clothes with any extra details you might want (I put in a few extra wrinkles in his jeans and, on his T-shirt, some stitches and a design.)

5 Go over the lines you want to keep in harder pencil so you can see them better, then ink in the drawing. Now the only thing left to do is...

Here are some more examples.....

...color him in!

Faces 2

Faces

The most important feature of any character is its face, and this is also the part that shows off your style of drawing the most. There are lots of different styles for drawing faces, and it would be impossible for me to describe them all. Instead, we'll see what makes one style different from another, and how you can get that into your own work. It's much better to try out lots of different ways of doing things in order to develop your own unique style of drawing!

Eyes

The most complicated part of the face has to be the eyes, and even they aren't too difficult once you get the hang them. So this is a good place to start. One of the main things that sets different styles apart is the artist's way of drawing them. We're going to start with a basic eye that, with practice, you can adapt to get any kind of eye you want. There are three main angles you have to learn: from the front, from the side, and from what is called "three-quarter" view, which is between the front and side views. This is one of the most important views to learn because most drawings will use this technique.

So let's draw some eyes. Remember to work lightly in pencil.

three-quarter side front
view

1 First draw the guidelines. The guidelines for the front and side views can be straight. For the three-quarter view (and for some other angles), they should be curved. Imagine them as if they were wrapped around a sphere. The side view does not need a vertical line.

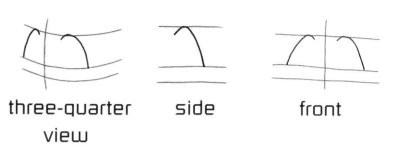

three-quarter side front
view

2 Next, draw a curve for the top of the eye, going from the middle line to the top one, and then down again. On the side and three-quarter views, the eye farthest away should be thinner than the one nearest. This curve is the eyelid.

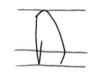

three-quarter side front
view

3 Now draw the lower part of the outside of the eye, as shown. Next, draw the unfinished oval that will be the iris. How much you leave out will depend on how large you want the shine on the eye to be.

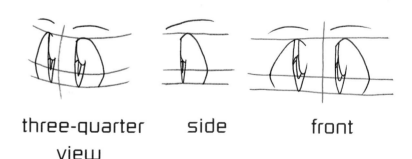

three-quarter side front
view

4 Add in the shine on the eye with another curve, as shown. Draw the pupils, and mark off a section in the eye to be darker. Put another line underneath this. Draw the eyebrows, which should be a straight line or even a simple curve. Experiment with drawing eyebrows—they take practice to get right.

5 Thicken the eyebrows where necessary, and add more ovals of shine to the eye. Then shade the areas that need shading, and thicken the outside of the eye. Here are some girls' eyes:

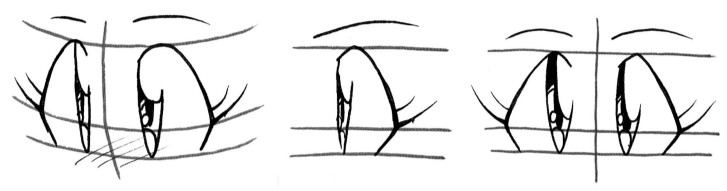

Here are some boys' eyes:

 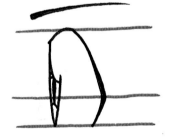 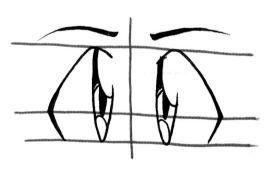

Some boys' eyes also have eyelashes drawn in, but they are not as obvious as on the girls' eyes. I've left the lashes off for these eyes.

19

Coloring the eye

Now it's time to try some
coloring. Draw another, large
eye to practice with.

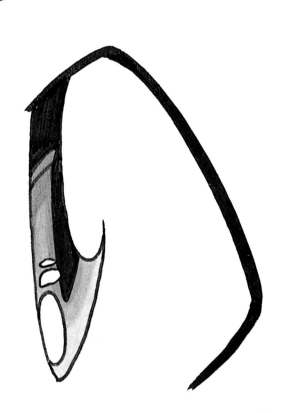

Color most of the iris a medium shade of whatever color you want the
eye to be – in this case, I used green – leaving a section at the bottom
a lighter, brighter shade of the same color. Use a darker shade of the
main color underneath the black section. You can also put a little of
this color around the pupil and at the edge of the eye farthest from
the main part of shine if you like. In many drawings, the artist will
blend the colors together even more.

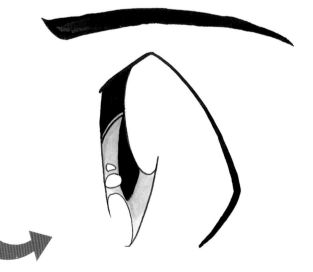

Now that you know the basics of how to draw an eye, you can see that it's made up of a number of different parts. There's the eyelid, the side of the eye, the iris, and the pupil. In some drawing styles you might draw in the lower eyelid. Let's look at how you can change the eyes to get a different look.

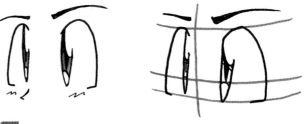

1 These are pretty similar to the basic eyes you've already learned to draw. However, the top eyelid is drawn from the top eye line right down to the lower one, instead of to the middle line, and a short line is drawn from the eyelid along the lower eye line. The iris is usually quite thin in this kind of eye.

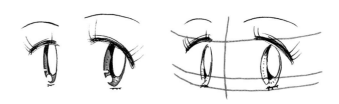

2 This style can be used to draw many different eyes. The eyelid does not go all the way to the middle line, but the corner joins it, and the side of the eye is quite high up. The eyelid curve is a lot flatter than in other kinds of eyes. Without thickening the line, this eye only really works on boys.

3 This is almost definitely a girl's eye. The eyelid is drawn with lots of thin lines and there is no defined "side" of the eye, as with the other styles on this page. The iris is a largish oval that is usually left partly covered. The shine on the iris usually has one BIG shine and at a least little one, if not more. There is often a lower lid drawn as well, as a little thin line with a few, very small, eyelashes coming off it. The eyebrows are drawn as thin lines, too.

4 This is a girl's eye, but with just one thin eyelash on each eye, or none at all, it could be made into a boy's eye. The eyelid goes to the normal place, but the side of the eye only goes about halfway to the lower eye line. This eye also has a lower lid, which is thin and quite pointed. The shine on the iris is a strange shape, and the black section is bigger. The eyelid has also been made quite thick.

5 This eye is very similar to the basic eye we started with, but is smaller in relation to the eyebrow, and a little more angular. A good rule of thumb is that the smaller the eyes, the farther apart they should seem. This eye can be made male or female in just the same way as the basic eye.

Starting to Construct the Face

Now you've got the most complicated part out of the way, it's time to take a closer look at how the face works. In the first chapter, you learned how to make a simple face from a circle, but most faces are shaped more like an egg (1-3.)

1

The pointed part is at the bottom front and forms the chin. Just have a look at these faces and you'll get the idea.

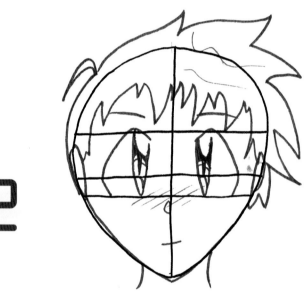

2

As you can see in the three-quarter view (4) when the face is tilted, the guidelines become curves instead of straight lines because the egg is round, and not flat. Remember: if you want things to look solid and not flat, you have to imagine them that way.

3

4

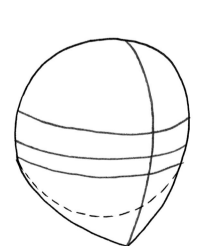

You've already got the basic idea of drawing faces from the front, so on the next page we'll try using an egg instead of a circle.

Face From the Front

Because you're still learning, try to copy this as closely as you can the first time. After that, you can start changing its appearance using what you learn.

1 Start off with your egg. This person is looking straight ahead, so none of the guidelines need to be curved. Look closely at the drawing to see where to put the eye lines. Think about what size the character's eyes should be when you do this.

2 Start to draw in the eyes and eyebrows. We've already covered this in depth so you should have no trouble.

3 Finish off the eyes and eyebrows. I wanted this face to be a girl, so I gave her some long eyelashes. Draw a little line for the nose and make the egg more face-shaped, as you did when it was a circle. This should be easy with this egg – you just need to make it more angular.

4 Give the face some small ears. You can't really see the ears well from this angle. Also, she's going to need a mouth. This should go about halfway between the nose and the bottom of the chin. I put in the hairline, too. Look at your own hairline to get the idea.

5 Next, draw her hair. As you can see, it took me a few attempts to get it how I wanted, but it's easy to redo. I also gave her a neck.

6 Now go over the lines you want to keep to see them better, and shade in any parts that you want to be darker when you ink in. Add some blush lines, too. Just draw a bunch of thin, light lines in the area around the nose. It doesn't matter if they go into the eyes.

7 Now go over the lines with ink. I've put extra shadows in the hair and little lines (called crosshatching) to show darker areas. Try and get different line weights in the drawing. The thinnest should be the blush lines and the thickest should be around the edge of the drawing.

8 This is what it would look like if I wanted to color it in. Notice the hair at the back is a darker color because it would be in the shadow.

You probably have the hang of drawing faces from the front by now. Let's move on to the most important view: the three-quarter view.

Face From Three-quarter View

This really isn't all that different from drawing from other angles. You do everything in about the same order, it's just that the way you do them is a little bit different each time.

3 Make the egg more facelike. Do the side farthest away from you in just the same way you would for a face from the front. On the other side, just draw in part of the chin. Do this lightly and you can adjust it once you draw the ear. Add in the nose, too. Finish off the eyes as well.

1 Start off with the kind of egg shape shown here. The guidelines are curved – imagine you have taken an egg and drawn the lines all the way around it. If you looked at it from an angle, the lines would be curved.

2 Draw in the eyes, just as you've been practicing. Use the guidelines to help you get them aligned properly.

6 Add any more details you might want and make the lines darker.

4 Draw the ear. The middle should be on the center eye line, as you can see. Give the guy a mouth, too. Next, I drew in the neck and the hairline.

5 Draw the hair. I put a few extra lines on the neck as well.

7 Ink it in and, if you want...

8 ...color it!

This view can be used in lots of ways, and it's a good idea to practice a few times. Try drawing some of these faces.

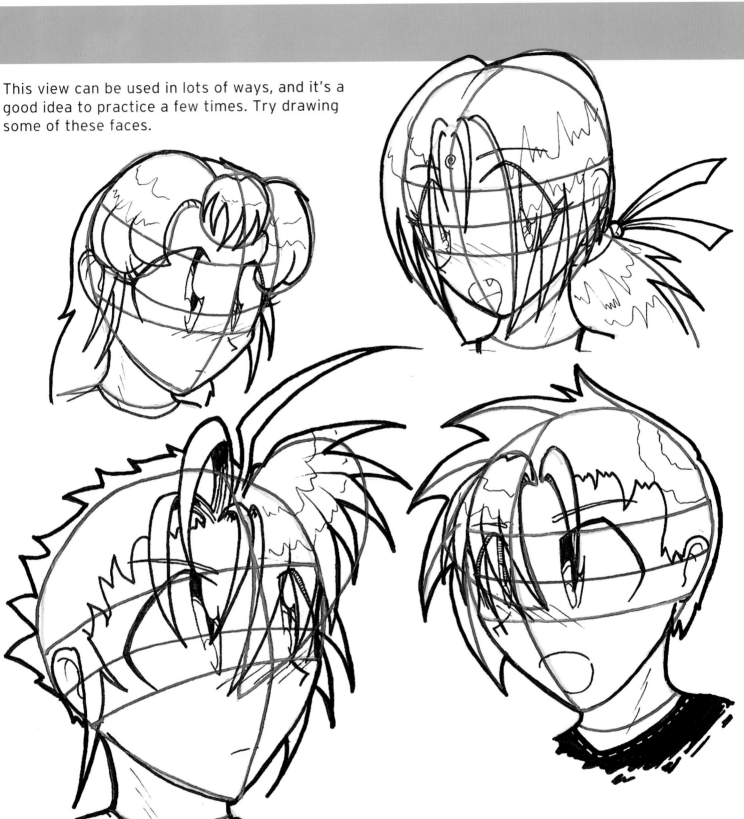

Now you've got the hang of that, there's a part of the face we should really have another look at before moving on to the side view.

Noses

There are several different ways of drawing a nose, and here are some of the easiest and most used ones.

1 This is the most common kind of nose. As you can see, it's like a checkmark standing on end.

2 This one is like the checkmark, but without the shorter line. It works well for when you don't want the nose to be very noticeable.

3 This is the kind of nose often used for Manga girls. It's very small and is sometimes drawn as just a little dot.

This is also drawn from the front. It's like a thick checkmark shape, but with the side that'll be in the middle of the face almost flat. The dark part should be on the side farthest from the light.

4 This nose is drawn like the last nose, but from the front. Here you make the upside-down "u" shape darker and the line in the middle much lighter.

5

6 This nose is also kind of like the first one, but looks more turned up. Draw it with the top line like the first kind of nose and a little upside-down "u" shape for the bottom.

Now you know some more ways of doing noses, try different combinations of eyes and noses.

Face From the Side ▶▶

This is probably the hardest view to get right, and you can only get it with practice. Copy what I have done here as closely as you can. Remember, if something doesn't look right to you, then you can always erase it and try again.

1 As you can see, the point of the egg shape is toward the front. There is no vertical guideline – you wouldn't be able to see it as it's normally drawn down the center of the face – and the eye lines are usually straight.

2 Draw in the eye.

3 Now draw the face shape. This is the hardest part to get the hang of, but once you have, it's very easy. The line should go out at the top eye line, come in toward the middle one, and go out again to the lower one. It continues out to the point of the nose. The curve should be rounded and smooth. Draw a flatter line from the point of the nose to the chin, and finish off the chin as you did in the three-quarter view.

4 Draw in the ear, the neck, and the hairline. Also give him a mouth.

5 Draw the hair.

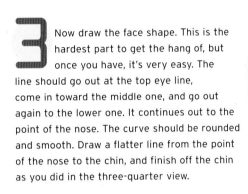

6 Add any more detail you want and pick out the lines you want to keep.

7 Ink it in, and finally...

8 ...color it.

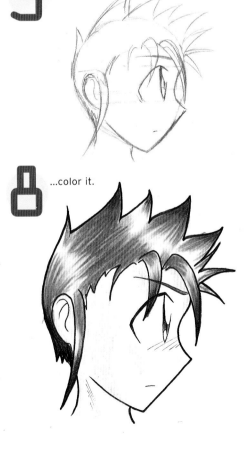

Now you can draw a face from all of the most important angles. Before we move on though, let's take a closer look at mouths from the side.

Face From the Side

There are a quite a few ways of drawing the mouth from the side. It can be quite difficult since you have to figure out how you want the lips to look.

In some drawings, such as this one, the lip isn't shown and the line of the face is drawn as if there was no mouth at all.

However, in this one, a gap is left where the lips would be. When thin lines are being used, this gap works well and your eyes fill in the rest of the detail.

Sometimes the artist likes to show the lips. A good way to do this is as in the previous drawing, but before the gap in the line it curves out a little, as shown here.

Often you need to show a character with its mouth open. You can do this without drawing all of the lines of the mouth.

In some Manga, the edge of the face isn't drawn solid.

Some show it much more boldly, drawing the whole shape of the mouth, but with a little bit missing, to make more than just a shape.

Hair

In the world of Anime and Manga, there is a wide range of weird and wonderful styles.

1

Drawing hair is usually done in three stages: the main body of the hair, the bangs, and any other part you might want to add on, like pony tails, braids, "ear-tails," and buns.

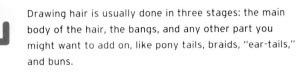

2

Think of bangs as a mass of curved, pointed shapes. Look at the drawings of the shapes. Just draw lots of bangs, nice and loosely. When drawing hair, you should let yourself go a little.

3

Here are some faces with different hairstyles for you to try. You don't have to draw the heads, just add the red lines to some faces you've done already and draw the rest of the hair. It's important to keep it nice and loose, and unless your style is very angular, nothing should be in a straight line. Try some of these.

To help you draw the main body of hair, think about how your own hair looks. If you have a part, all of your hair runs from that (d). Many Manga characters have spiked hair, and this tends to follow a set of lines from a point near the back of the head (b).

When drawing hair, it helps to visualize these lines to help you see how the hair should flow and what direction to use when you color it.

When you're just starting out, it's a good idea to draw these lines in first. If the bangs stick out in front of the hair, I do those first and then draw the rest of the hair afterward (a&c).

(a)

(b)

(c)

(d)

Inking Hair

For most parts of a drawing, you have to be careful and accurate, but when it comes to the hair, it looks much better if you work quickly. Practice making thick and thin lines and drawing quick, smooth curves. Above all, be confident. If you worry too much about each little line being perfect, the art will look too awkward. It's your drawing, so however you do it will be right.

Have a look at some of these hairstyles and see if you can draw them.

1

This guy is pretty simple, with a few bangs at the front and the rest of his hair sweeping forward.

2

This girl has a lot of braids. Small braids are easy to draw.

All you need are two sets of little curves.

Draw them quickly and freely, overlapping each curve slightly, and you'll get a great-looking braid in no time.

3

This is a little more complicated, but not as hard as it looks. It was made from lots of shapes like this one...

5

4

This guy has pretty wild bangs with lots of points. There are quite a few thin hairs in there, too, drawn with one line and flicking the pen off at the end.

This girl's hair is pretty simple. The big bangs are made up of three of the usual shapes run together. You can give people some wild-shaped bangs as long they are not thicker at the bottom than the top.

Other Angles

When drawing characters, you might want them to be looking up or down or to have their heads tilted in some other way.

This is usually pretty simple. You just draw the guidelines, then draw the face around them.

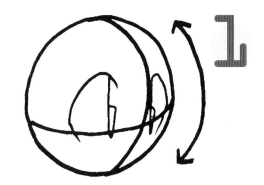

You can turn the head up and down (1-3).

As well as tilting it toward or away from you (4-7).

Try drawing some of these – I left the guidelines in to help you.

Expressions

Eye expression

Now that you know how to construct a face, it's time to learn how to draw different expressions.

There are three parts of the face you can change to make different expressions. You can change the eyes, eyebrows, and mouth.

You actually get most of the expression from the eyebrows, but there are some things you can change about the way you draw the eyes to show how your character is feeling.

1 The first is to change the size of the iris and pupil.

2 If you make the iris and the pupil smaller, the character will look more surprised. This works especially well from a side view.

3 You can make a character look tired by drawing his or her eyes part-closed, like this.

4 A character whose eyebrows cover some of the eyes, will look very angry.

5 Giving the eyes a lot of shine will make the character look like he or she's about to cry.

6 Changing the direction the character is looking can change his or her mood, especially if he or she is staring into space. Looking up tends to make a character appear more hopeful and absent, whereas looking down creates a worried or ashamed look.

7 Making the pupil small or...

8 ...leaving it out altogether makes your character look dazed, or maybe hypnotized, if the story calls for it.

33

Closed eyes

Closed eyes can give you different expressions as well, and these rely on the eyebrow even more.

1 Most closed eyes curve either up or down. If the edges curve down, it usually means the expression is stronger.

2 These eyes could be happy or sad. This person looks calm.

3 Drawing one eye closed will mean your character is winking.

4 This person is angry, but is controlled about it. The expression is not as strong as when the edges of the eye curve down.

5 These eyes make the character look very angry about something. He is probably about to shout at someone.

6 You can draw someone screwing up his or her eyes in pain or in really great anger by having all the lines point toward a place between the eyes.

7 In little Chibi drawings, you can have characters looking happy by drawing upside-down "U" shapes for the eyes, like this. It doesn't work so well on more serious drawings, but on fun ones I think it looks really cute.

8 Another Chibi style - drawing crosses for eyes is a way of showing someone who is unconscious.

Eyebrows

Eyebrows really are the most important part of the face for showing expression. It takes practice, but just a slight change in the way you draw the eyebrow can finish off any expression perfectly. Here are some basic eyebrows to use in your drawings. For each one, the eye is exactly the same – it's just the eyebrow that changes. You can really see the difference, can't you?

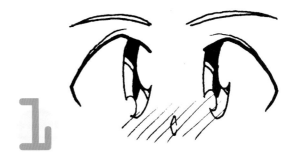

1 This is just a plain, normal pair of eyebrows, the kind you'd use for most smiles. They should get thinner toward the outside of the eye and be slightly curved. It's pretty rare for eyebrows to be straight – just take a look in the mirror.

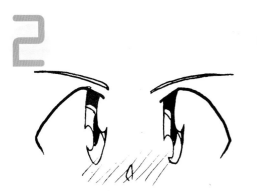

2 This one looks a little annoyed. You can achieve it by making the eyebrows angle down at the middle. The steeper the line, the angrier the face will seem.

3 This character looks worried. The eyebrows are angled up at the middle and are not as curved. If you want the face to look even more worried, you could curve the eyebrows a little.

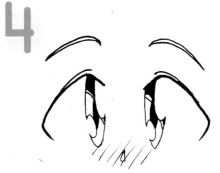

4 Eeek! This face looks like the character just got a surprise. You draw it by making the eyebrows curved and high up above the eye.

5 This person looks confused or suspicious. You can do it by having one brow look a little annoyed and the other more shocked and higher up.

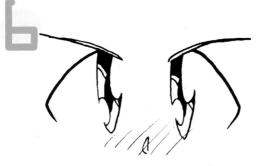

6 This person looks very angry. His eyebrows are pointed so far down, they touch his eyes.

Once you practice these and try them with different eyes, you'll master these expressions in no time!

Mouths

The last important part of the face is the mouth. On these drawings, the eyes are covered up and the mouth is drawn in dark so you can see it better.

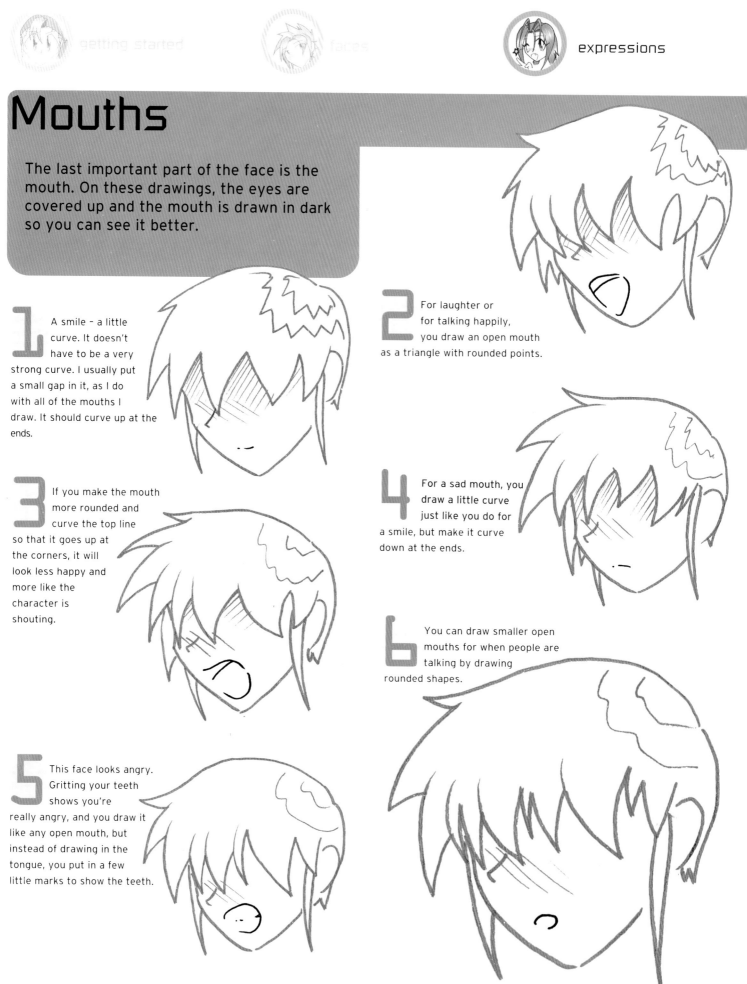

1 A smile – a little curve. It doesn't have to be a very strong curve. I usually put a small gap in it, as I do with all of the mouths I draw. It should curve up at the ends.

2 For laughter or for talking happily, you draw an open mouth as a triangle with rounded points.

3 If you make the mouth more rounded and curve the top line so that it goes up at the corners, it will look less happy and more like the character is shouting.

4 For a sad mouth, you draw a little curve just like you do for a smile, but make it curve down at the ends.

5 This face looks angry. Gritting your teeth shows you're really angry, and you draw it like any open mouth, but instead of drawing in the tongue, you put in a few little marks to show the teeth.

6 You can draw smaller open mouths for when people are talking by drawing rounded shapes.

Examples of Expression

Now that you have all the basics, let's take a look at how you can put them together to get different expressions. It's up to you to pick which features suit what is happening in your picture, and here are some ideas.

1 This is a blank expression. The flat mouth and eyebrows make the face look worried.

2 Angry eyebrows and an open mouth make him look like he's telling someone off, or maybe talking.

3 Surprised eyebrows, taller eyes with small pupils, and a small, round mouth make a person look like he's just seen, something surprising. Giving him extra blush lines makes him look embarrassed, too.

4 Part-closed eyes, annoyed eyebrows, and a slightly downward-curving mouth make a character look bored and annoyed. He looks suspicious of what he has seen. Whatever it is, he is not amused.

5 A happy, open mouth and neutral eyebrows make him look as if he's happy to tell somebody something, and maybe a little excited.

6 Worried eyebrows, lots of blush lines, and an open, but sad, mouth make him look very upset. Little blue-and-white tears at the edges of his eyes make him look as if he's about to cry. Awww!

7 Worried eyebrows, eyes that look down, and a wobbly line for the mouth, along with lots of blush lines, will make a character look very embarrassed and ashamed.

8 This guy is making some NOISE. Angry eyebrows and closed eyes, as well as a big, open mouth, show that he's shouting loudly.

9 Eeeeek! With surprised, worried eyebrows, huge eyes, with small, shocked pupils, and a big, open mouth, he must have seen something shocking. Tear shapes around his face and eyes show that it's scary, too!

And that's just about all you need to know about drawing faces. Now let's move on to drawing full figures...

Bodies

Bodies

Now that you've mastered drawing faces, it's time to look at how you draw bodies. Remember all that stuff about tubes and spheres way back in Chapter 1? They're what drawing bodies is all about!

You see, the body is made up of a collection of shapes, which get hidden as you put the detail over them 'and erase the pencil work.

The shapes you need for a body aren't all that complicated. Imagine it like a puppet or a mannequin, kind of like this.

Bodies

The body's almost all made up of tubes and spheres. But in order to get the shapes in the right places, you need something to draw them on to - a kind of skeleton. What we use for this is a stick figure.

Of course, this drawing is a bit TOO simple for what we want. We need a more realistic stick man. In order to get a more authentic body - as realistic as a stick man can be - he needs to have joints, just like you do. He needs shoulders, hips, knees, and elbows.

Draw a circle at each of the joints because they're very important. Try drawing these stick figures yourself. Doodle them whenever you can't think of anything else to draw, and try out different poses.

I'm sure you've seen stick men before, and I bet you've drawn them. You know, the little doodles that look something like this:

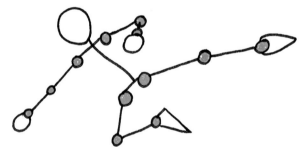

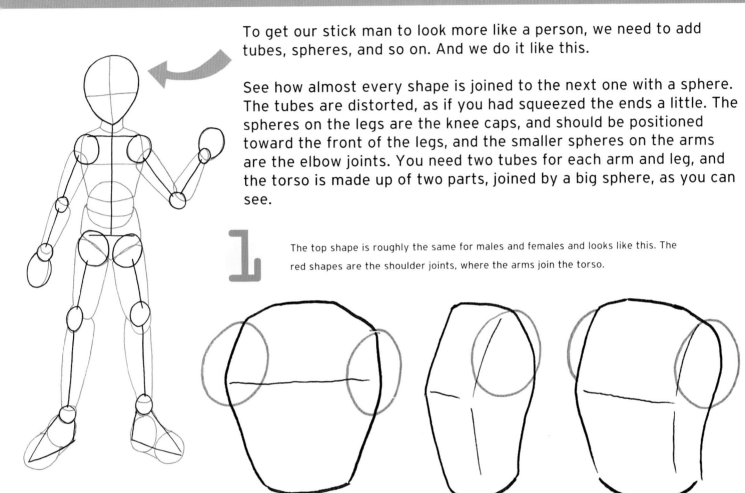

To get our stick man to look more like a person, we need to add tubes, spheres, and so on. And we do it like this.

See how almost every shape is joined to the next one with a sphere. The tubes are distorted, as if you had squeezed the ends a little. The spheres on the legs are the knee caps, and should be positioned toward the front of the legs, and the smaller spheres on the arms are the elbow joints. You need two tubes for each arm and leg, and the torso is made up of two parts, joined by a big sphere, as you can see.

1 The top shape is roughly the same for males and females and looks like this. The red shapes are the shoulder joints, where the arms join the torso.

front   side   three-quarter view

2 The lower part of the torso is a little different for male and female characters. The easiest way to think of it is like underwear. So on a girl it will be like this.

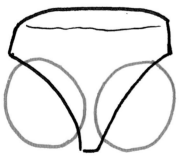  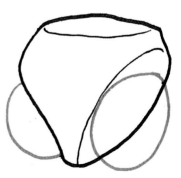

front   side   three-quarter view

Bodies

And on a boy it will be more like this.

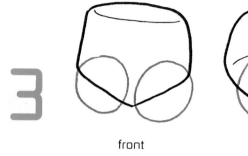

3

front   side   three-quarter view

The red shapes here are the joints the legs will join.

4 You also use tubes and spheres for the hands. Here's a close-up of an arm's different shapes so you can have a better look.

5 You don't need to draw all the shapes for the hands when you're designing the figure, just the main part of them. (We'll go over hands and feet in more detail later.) Practice drawing different arm positions (get a mirror and look at how your own arm works).

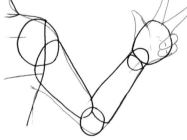

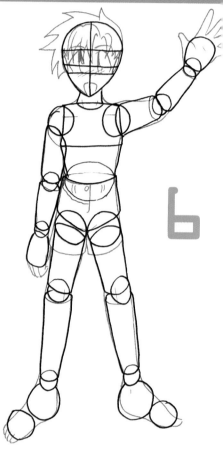

6

Once you get used to how the body goes together, you don't need to make the stick man very obvious. You just use the spheres and tubes to show the general shape and, on top of those, you draw the actual lines you want for the body, like this.

Remember that the spheres are the joints, so the tubes should only be able to move in such a way that they are still "touching" the spheres.

7 To draw the actual arm, you make the shapes a lot smoother when you go over them. (You should draw the basic shapes very lightly.) Fill in the gaps between the shapes so it looks like this.

8 The same goes for the legs.

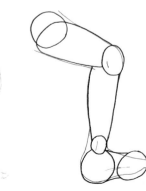

Hands and Feet

Hands are one of the hardest things to draw, but with practice, and the right start, anyone can get the hang of them.

It isn't very difficult. You start hands like this.

1

2

Add four spheres for the finger joints, a lump for the thumb, and a sphere for the thumb joint.

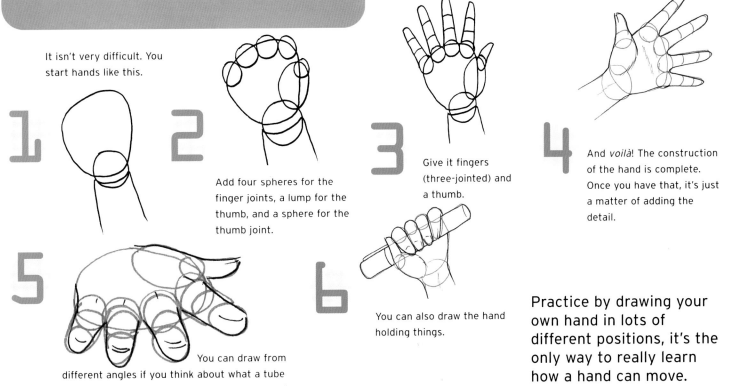

3

Give it fingers (three-jointed) and a thumb.

4

And *voilà*! The construction of the hand is complete. Once you have that, it's just a matter of adding the detail.

5

You can draw from different angles if you think about what a tube looks like when you turn it. (It gets shorter and you can see more of its end.) This is called foreshortening.

6

You can also draw the hand holding things.

Practice by drawing your own hand in lots of different positions, it's the only way to really learn how a hand can move.

The construction of the foot is pretty easy.

Under the ankle sphere, you have a big lump joined to a smaller one, with a bunch of little round-ended tubes for the toes.

If you turn it you can see the details better.

Drawing it from the front can sometimes be a little difficult, but if you think it through, it's not really all that hard. Just remember where everything goes.

Of course, most of the time you're not going to need to draw the toes in any detail because the shoes will be in the way.

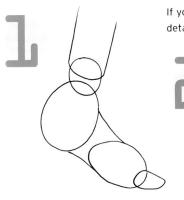

1

2

3

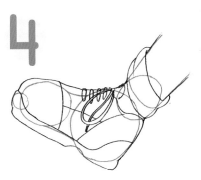

4

Bodies and Proportions

You draw boys and girls a little differently. It's not all that important when you're just starting out, but a guy's shoulders would be wider and his body should, in general, go almost straight down (only if he's standing straight, obviously.) A girl should have wider hips and everything should be more curved. Her waist should be thinner and more obvious than a guy's, and when she stands, her knees should be closer together than a guy's.

Good proportions are difficult to achieve, so in most cases there are a few rules that you should apply.

When standing straight, with your arms by your side, your elbows fall to your waist and your hands go about halfway down your upper legs.

One other thing is that for animation, the "shorter" the proportions are, the bigger the character's eyes should generally be.

Let's have a look at some different proportions.

1

In more serious Anime, characters have more realistic proportions. They're about six heads high. Their eyes are fairly small, as are their feet and hands.

4

You can't take things of this kind of proportion too seriously. The boy is in Chibi (three heads tall) and the girl is in even more extreme Chibi style – not much taller than two heads high. The eyes are huge because they're both so short.

2

3

These characters are pretty standard for kids. They're just under four heads high, although, because the girl is standing on tiptoe, she looks taller.

These characters are drawn in about five-head-height proportion. They look very cartoonlike, but not too much, and the eyes are bigger. I use this technique quite often.

Drawing Your First Full Body ▶▶

Now that you've got the theory out of the way, it's time to draw your first serious, full figure.

Here are two people in easy poses. I suggest you draw one of them, following the steps, then come back and do the second one afterward. Because this is your first attempt, try to copy almost exactly what you see, and remember to work very lightly until near the end. There are many lines you won't want to keep in final drawings, so you need to make sure they're faint enough not to get in the way of the lines you do want.

1 Start off with your stick figure. Both characters are standing sideways, although the figure on the right, who will be male, is slightly turned away, and the figure on the left, who will be a girl, is turned slightly toward us.

2 Add your shapes and start on the face. You don't need to draw the parts that are hidden by the rest of the body. You don't need to be super-neat, either. I tend to be very sketchy at this stage. When you get confident, you can skip the first step altogether and do all your planning just with the shapes.

3 Now start to add the detail. Draw in the hands and start to smooth out the shapes. Make a start on the clothes.

4 The clothes are loose and so they hang off the body. That means the top of the guy's sleeve should be at the top of his arm and the bottom should hang underneath.

5 I pushed his T-shirt up at the back, like this, and because it's all rumpled up, I made it seem thicker at the ends and added a line to show that it's creased at the front.

6 This is how you do creases. Where the fabric is bunched together, you draw lines going toward the bend. Where things are pushing against the fabric, you draw checkmark shapes going away from whatever is doing the pushing.

7 Now add even more detail. I put in the trims and decorations on their clothes, finished the hands, feet, and faces, and added more detail to the hair. Keep working until everything's just the right shape. If it doesn't look quite right, you don't have to erase it if you've only drawn it lightly: you can just add more lines over the top until it looks correct to you.

Draw the clothes and add in detail to the face. Draw in the basic shapes for the hair.

Drawing Your First Full Body

8

Now go over the lines you want to keep with a heavier pencil. Your drawing may look a little messy at this point, but make sure you can see everything that you want to keep. I shaded in the girl's top as I was getting ideas for which colors to use, but it's going to be erased, so it's not important.

9

Now ink in the drawing. I did the really fine details – the decoration on the clothes and the features in the faces – in my thinnest pen (0.1) and inked the rest in a medium-sized pen (0.3). Then I went over the outside of the figures in a slightly thicker pen (0.5). Making the outline of the drawing thicker makes it stand out more on the page. It always makes things look much more interesting if you use a big variety of line thickness in your art. It also looks good if you make some parts thicker where shadows would be. Sometimes you'll get ideas for little details on the clothes as you ink, or maybe even after you've rubbed out the pencil lines. For me, it was the stitches on the girl's skirt and the ends of the ribbons in her hair. When that happens, you can go back and sketch them in, or, if you're feeling confident, you can draw them straight in with pen.

10

Once it's inked, you can color it. I chose nice, bright colors for the girl and a slightly calmer color scheme for the boy.

Action Shots

Now you've got the hang of how you draw a basic figure, let's try a more complicated pose. We're going to draw an action shot.

1 Start off with the stick figure again. When you draw one of your own, think about how the character moves. If you have trouble thinking of how a pose should go, use your own body to get a feel for it.

2 Now put on the basic shape. I drew in all of the back leg, but made the part we won't be able to see in the final drawing faint. This was to make sure both legs looked right.

4 Here I finished off all the details. I decided the sleeves of his T-shirt should be caught by the wind and blowing back, as well as the cuffs of his gloves, so I changed them to show that. I added more creases in his clothes, decoration on his trainers, and the rest of the detail to his face and hair. I then went over any lines that weren't clear so that I could see them, and...

3 Once you have the basic shapes, it's time to start adding detail. Because the figure is in the air, I made the edge of his T-shirt blow in the wind. The character is also going to have the ends of his headband flying out behind him.

5 ...inked it in. Like last time, when I inked in the drawing I went over the outside with a thicker pen. I also added shadows in the cuffs, shirtsleeves, under his shirt, and on the cuff of his pants. After that...

6 ...I colored him in. I made the colors fairly bright and gave him green eyes to contrast with his reddish-brown hair.

Poses and Actions

When drawing people, you have to decide how exaggerated you want the pose to be. If it's someone on the move, it's almost always best to draw the most extreme position, as well as using other tricks, to show the speed and movement. For instance:

In this picture the character looks like he's running, but not very fast. It doesn't really look very dynamic at all. However...

1

2

...in this drawing he is obviously going much faster. This is far better – there is a greater feeling of movement. As well as having a strong pose, his clothes and hair are being blown back by the wind.

3

Using the wind is a very good way of showing movement and works especially well with characters with loose things in their costumes or long hair.

← wind →

4

If there is a lot of wind, things that hang should be blown in the direction of the breeze, like this.

5

Also, when a character moves fast, wind is shown in the opposite direction, like this.

movement

wind

← wind →

When choosing a pose for your character, think about his or her personality and how he or she moves. For instance, when walking, one character may strut along confidently, while another may wander along dejectedly, hanging his head and dragging his feet. The mood you show depends on the pose, as well as the facial expression. Try to imagine how you walk or stand in different moods.

The only way to get good at drawing poses, just like anything else, is to practice it. I have drawn a bunch of characters in different poses below, along with the stick figure I used to get the pose next to them. See if you can copy them.

Finishing Touches

Inking ▶▶

This poster-style image uses many different inking techniques. As you can see, it has two figures and, in the background, a big, menacing face, most likely belonging to the bad guy.

Inking

To get a good-looking image in pen, you need to practice different pen strokes.

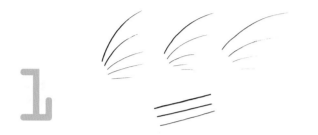

1 You can vary the thickness of the line with pressure or, in some cases, the angle you hold the pen. The size of pen you use will obviously make a difference, too.

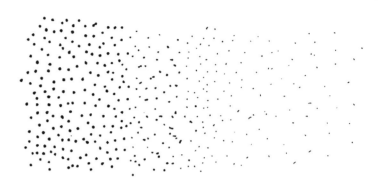

2 It's possible to get a form of shading in black and white using patterns of dots and lines. Drawing dots by hand is very tedious and takes a long time to cover a big area, but it can look very effective if used well.

3 This is a form of "crosshatching," and can be used to cover large areas. I used it for the background of the picture.

4 These shapes were made with a brush pen, though you should be able to do it with a paint brush, too, providing you don't load it with too much ink. This is how I did the "magic" effect around the boy's hand.

5 Crosshatching is a way of shading by using lines. To make it darker, you add more lines over the top in a different direction to the first ones. The technique gets its name from the way the lines cross over each other.

6 The thickness of lines helps to show distance. In general, the thicker the line, the closer the object is to you. It usually looks best to make the outline of any object thicker than all of the other lines because this makes the image look sharper.

Color

Here's another group shot, of a pair of "magical girls" and a mysterious boy.

The colors are very bright as they work well for this kind of picture.

 1

This is a color wheel. The colors sitting next to each other are called complementary colors. This means they go well together without detracting from each other. So red and orange are complementary, as are blue and purple.

See how the lead girl in the picture on the right wears mostly complementary colors – mainly red, orange, and yellow.

 2   3

The colors opposite each other on the wheel are contrasting colors. These show up well if you put them together, like this.

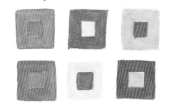

The blues and purples of the second girl contrast with the lead girl's oranges and yellows, and the blue-green background shows up the bright flames.

The more the subjects differ to the background color, the more they will stand out and will appear closer. If you make the subject duller, or more like the background color, it will look farther away.

WARM

4

COOL

Colors can be divided into two groups: warm and cool (or hot and cold). The colors closer to red and orange are warm, and the colors that are more blue are cool. Warm colors tend to be brighter. If you have many warm colors in the characters, it's best to use cold colors for the background, and vice versa, as this will make them stand out. You should usually make the characters brighter than the background so that people's attention is drawn to them.

Shading

This picture shows a character caught in a spotlight. The bright light shining on him makes the shadows and highlights in the picture much stronger.

If you think about what you know about color, you'll notice most of the background of this picture is a warm color (brick red) and the character's clothes are mainly in cold colors.

1

When coloring things, it's important to practice different tones or shades. First practice pressing lightly and then move on to pressing harder.

2

The most important thing to remember about shading is where the light is coming from. Things get darker the farther away from the light they are...

3

...no matter what shape they are. Many objects have a small, lighter line along the darkest edge - a highlight - and if you want, you can put this in.

4

The other important thing to remember is that things cast shadows on each other. Your picture will look more realistic if you put in the shadows.

5

If an object is wrinkled, or has a lot of curves in it, it may cast a shadow on itself and have extra highlights. It can be hard to figure these out, but practice, and use other pictures to help you decide where they should go.

Texture

This "sword and sorcery" picture has a mixture of hot and cold colors, but the thicker outlines around the characters at the front mean they don't blend into the background as well as the boy on the dragon does.

You can really be creative when thinking up animals and monsters as most are made from a few simple shapes, just like people are.

This dragon is easy. Just a few shapes, and after you've added detail to it...

1

2

...you have a dragon. You can experiment with many different spines and fins to make them look different. Other animals can be made in the same way once you've worked out what shapes you'll need. If you need help, try using a photograph or a book to base it on.

3 For the dragon, you'll need to draw scales. You do it like this. The body tends to be shiny, so make the edges darker. Once you've shaded it, add lots of little "u"' shapes for the scales - in black, if it's rough - or, as in most cases, in the same color as the body.

4

The leathery wings can be made by adding lines of a darker shade to the main color, as if they were shadows from lots of little creases.

5 For people, hair can be made to look more hairlike by adding a jagged, lighter patch where the light catches it. It'll look even better if the rest of the color is uneven, but make sure you keep all the lines going in the direction the hair is going.

It is useful to be able to draw gems and jewels. Round gems should be colored in much the same way as you color an eye, with a large shine. The color should be dark near the shine, becoming lighter farther away from the light.

6

7 Cut jewels can be drawn by shading each surface dark near the light, becoming lighter farther away from it.

8 Shiny, flat metal things have a strip of light on them, and the color is darker on either side of the light.

9 Like jewels, rounded metal gets darker toward the light.

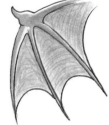

Background

As you know, things look smaller the farther away they are.

The way to get the background to look more realistic is to use a technique called perspective. Perspective is important, and it's well worth practicing until you can do it well.

The two most used kinds are called one-point perspective and two-point perspective.

Here's a picture with a "realistic" background. I decided it should be on a sunny day, so the colors are light and bright.

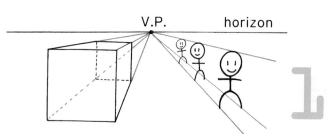

1

This is one-point perspective. All the lines go toward one point on the horizon, called a "vanishing point" (written as V.P. on the diagram). Draw the lines in lightly because you'll have to erase them later. Practice drawing boxes in perspective.

2

horizon

This is how the lines would look for a simple street. You use the lines to work out where the scenery should go.

3

V.P.   horizon   V.P.

This is two-point perspective. It is called that because it has two vanishing points.

4

When drawing the sky, it's usually darkest at the top and, most times in the day, gets lighter toward the horizon.

5

These objects are fairly simple.. They're all made of easy shapes.

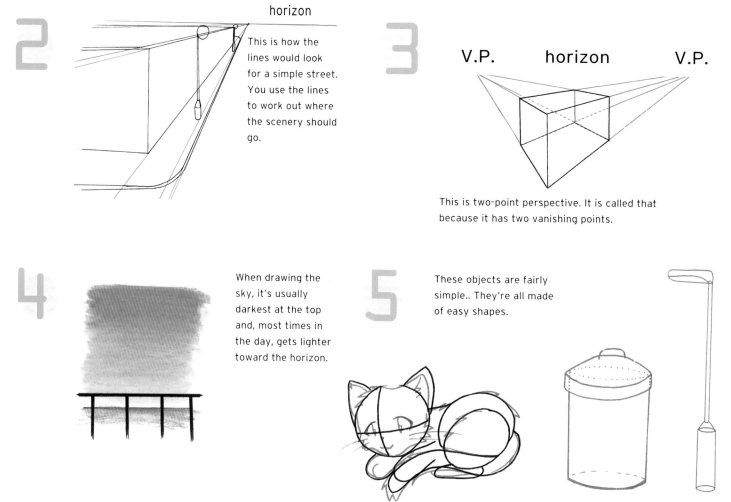

It can take a while to learn to do, but if you practice and think of things in terms of boxes (called "crating"), they can be put in easily.

Atmosphere

In these pictures, the boy is dreaming about someone. Maybe you can think of a story to go with the pictures – I had one in mind when I drew them.

When drawing pictures to tell a story, you can create different moods with color and background and the way you use them.

The night can be a special time, and a shooting star can make the night seem even more special.

Bright colors and blue skies are summery.

Warm colors make things seem warm and comforting, maybe even romantic. Cherry blossoms (*sakura*) are a common image in both Anime and Manga.

Using mostly blue makes the picture seem sad, especially if you color the whole picture in a light layer of blue before working on top of it. Rain adds to the mood as well.

Think of the images that mean the most to you, and try putting them in your art. The more care and thought you put into your characters, the better they will look. I always like to have a story behind the pictures I draw and, if you do it well, people should be able to see that there is a story behind your art, too.

Materials

Materials

There are many different drawing materials available and, if you want to draw, there are some things you really cannot do without. Of course, there are also things you don't need, but are fun to experiment with anyway! Start with some good-quality stuff to get you off on the right foot.

Here are the basics.

Pencils

You've got two main choices here: mechanical pencils and the traditional kind. Your best bet will probably be to get a couple of each, particularly the traditional kind. Personally, I like using mechanical pencils because they're clean and you don't have to sharpen them. All you do is refill the lead once in a while. A good mechanical pencil can cost a lot, but it will last a long time. There are different kinds of lead available for them, too. I tend to use 0.7 and 0.5 leads because they're pretty thin, but not as expensive as 0.35 or thinner.

You can buy traditional pencils with different types of lead, from more than 11H (very hard) to BB (very, very, soft and black). It's best to have a selection of them because each one has a different purpose. A soft pencil is good for getting varying tones, but it does smudge easily and can make a mess if you're not careful. Hard pencils are much cleaner and lighter. You'll most likely want a 2H, HB, and 2B, along with maybe something softer, like a 6B or 7B.

Paper

The kind of paper you use usually depends on the type of image you want. Most of the time you'll want a fairly smooth paper. I tend to buy myself a ream of fairly good-quality photocopy paper. It might seem expensive, but it'll last a long time. I also use cartridge-paper sketchbooks because they're easy to carry around. Try to find one with a good, strong backing board so you won't have to bother carrying a drawing board or book to lean on. Another thing you might want to get is a sketchbook with a more textured paper. This isn't good for ink, but great for pencils.

Pens

There are many different kinds of pens for inking, and one thing you should almost always go for is "pigment ink." Pigment ink, also known as India ink, is special because once it's dry, it'll stay where you put it. In other words, you can use paint, colored inks, markers, and pretty much whatever else you want without having to worry about the black bleeding into your colors and making them look dirty.

Fine-liners

These are some of the best pens to have when you're starting out. They come in various nib sizes and are clean and easy to use. Make sure you don't get a roller-ball pen because they tend to smudge very easily. It's best to have a good collection of nib sizes. I usually keep a 0.1 for really fine lines, a 0.3 for general work, and a 0.5 or 0.8 for thicker lines. Try out different brands – I like the kind that gives you a thin line that becomes thicker as you press harder. These pens come in many colors, and you can get some really interesting effects. Try out a few sepia (a reddish-brown color) fine-liners or other unusual colors.

Dip-pens

These are used by professional artists. You can get much more variety in line thickness with these, but they are harder to use.

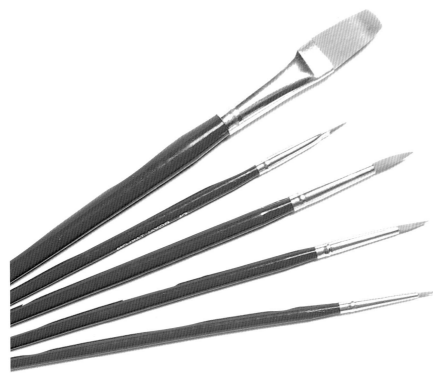

Brushes

These are also fun. Many professionals use brushes, but they do take a lot of getting used to. A good brush or brush pen will give you varying thickness, as long as you keep it in good condition. It takes time, patience, and a lot of practice to use one, but you can get some really great results, and they're fun to use.

Pencil Sharpener

A metal one is best, preferably one with two different sharpening ends. You can sharpen chalks, wax crayons, and pastels in the larger end.

Ballpoint Pen

These pens aren't so good for inking, and I tend to avoid them if I can. However, you can get some nice "sketch" effects with them.

Ruler

Most rulers are pretty much the same – just make sure yours is longer than the size of paper you normally use. Try to use your ruler as little as possible, and practice drawing straight lines without it – most things in life aren't really straight, after all. The only things you should really need a ruler for is drawing frames on a comic or borders and some special effects.

Erasers

A good eraser is essential. The best ones I've found are plastic erasers, which work very well and don't lift off your ink. Kneadable erasers are also very good, though they do tend to get dirty easily. A benefit of these erasers is that you can make them into any shape you want to take out small areas. Another kind of eraser is a little harder to find – but if you can find a good one I recommend getting one – and that is an eraser "pencil." They're just like normal pencils, but instead of having a lead, they have a strip of eraser that you can actually sharpen and use to get to very delicate parts of your picture. This is really useful if you like leaving your work in pencil. Eraser pencils that you sharpen by tearing off a strip of paper instead of using a normal pencil sharpener are even better. I use mine all the time.

Materials

Well, that's the most important stuff, and we haven't even started on color yet! Here are some ideas of color media to try.

Markers

There are two main kinds here: permanent markers and water-based markers. The former tend to be very expensive, but they work really well. They do take a lot of getting used to, so it's something you'll need to practice a lot. Water-based makers are more commonly known as "felt pens." They're quick and bright, but often have a limited choice of color. However, if you use a washable brand, you can use water with them to get a "watercolor" effect.

Paint

Most paint can be classified as either transparent or opaque. Opaque media normally needs to be used on thick paper or canvas. Acrylics, oils, gouache, and poster paints are all opaque. Watercolors, on the other hand, are transparent. They can be used on thin paper, as well as over the top of other media, but work better over liquid media rather than pencils. They're most often used for doing subtle shades and washes.

Colored pencils

These are often overlooked, but are very nice to work with. You can get a huge variety of tone and color with them, blending and overlaying them. Regular colored pencils are very good for fine detail and thin lines, like hair. You can even work over the top of other media with them. Try to get fairly good-quality ones, preferably those that "blend." Another really neat kind of pencil is the "watercolor" pencil. You can use it like a normal colored pencil or, by adding water on top of it, you can get a watercolor effect. I use these quite often, especially for doing skin. You can also get special markers that blend normal pencils as if they were watercolor pencils.

Inks

As well as the black India ink you'll use with your marking pens, you can get many different colors of bottled ink. The colors tend to be very bright and concentrated so you can get really vivid colors. I like to use them over the top of other media or as a base for other more detailed media.

Pastels

You can buy these in chalk or oil versions. They are good for large pieces, but for small work they get quite difficult to work with. Pastel dust can be used to create some interesting backgrounds, though.

Computer

If you have a scanner, you can think about using computer coloring, but we won't go into that in this book. You can experiment with it and get some amazing effects.

Index

Dedications and Thank-you's

This book is for anyone who has ever looked at a picture and wondered "How DID they do that?"

Thanks and hugs go to:

Mom and Dad - you know why. Words can't even touch it.

Hayley, Chandra, Dean, Philip, and Jack "Dave" James (in no particular order) - cheers guys. You've supported me, cheered me on, and been there for me when I needed it most. I couldn't have done this without you - I love you all.

Everyone else: there are too many of you to mention, but you all know who you are. Anyone who's given me the slightest word of encouragement, I'm grateful to you all. Thanks for putting up with me. But in case you don't know, some of you are Ben, Val, Sam, Carla, Cerys, Jo, and Fiona.

Thank you also to David and Sarah, without whom this would never have happened. Thanks for giving me a chance.